WELCOME ABOARD

Welcome to Cooking on the Guiding Light. My name is Shane and I have owned the Guiding Light for over nine years with the last seven running charters in the Virgin Islands. On my charters I cook three dinners a week for my guests and over the years I have had many of them tell me I should write a cookbook, so that is what I finally did.

But Cooking on the Guiding Light is more than just recipes, I want to entertain you with some of my stories and adventures. So, the beginning of each category will start with a story. Some of them are supposed to make you laugh and others help you understand life aboard a boat. As far as tying them to each category, some were really easy and others I made some quick turns. I hope you find that just as entertaining.

Before we start, let me tell you a little about myself. I bought the Guiding Light in 2009 and started cruising at the beginning of 2010. That first year I cruised from Houston all the way to Nantucket. In 2011 I sailed throughout the Bahamas and Turks & Caicos. From there, St Thomas in the US Virgin Islands and where I started my charter business in 2012. Since then I have sailed the Caribbean islands and during the hurricane season (Aug-Nov), I haul my boat out of the water and spend my time traveling.

Travel is my passion and I love sharing it with my guests and on my website (www.svGuidingLight.com) through my blogs, photos, podcasts, travel videos, and travel guides where I talk and write about anything and everything sailing, cruising, and travel related. My two biggest goals right now are to sail around the world and also visit every country. I figure with these goals even if I fail I will have the time of my life.

I try and live my life and inspire others with the following mottos:
1) "You cannot change the direction of the wind, but you can adjust the trim of your sail" - meaning life will throw at you whatever it wants. It is up to you to weather the storm in order to achieve your dreams.
2) "The difference between an adventure and an ordeal is attitude" - this one comes from Bob Bitchin at Cruising Outpost and it means you can choose to accept and make the best of whatever circumstance you find yourself in or not.
3) "Experience is the thing you gain right after you needed it" - this is my way of saying do not let inexperience and fear stop you from following your dreams.

With all that said, I hope my writings entertain you and also inspires you to follow your dreams. I will now sign off and let you get to the reason you got this book in the first place. May you have fair winds and following seas.

Capt. Shane McClellan

Table of Contents

COCKTAILS

Recently I was asked how I came up with my "Da Lime In Da Coconut" drink recipe. It all came about at the beginning of my second-year chartering. I was doing my famous "Captain's Drink of the Day" but needed more recipes. I heard of a drink called Da Lime In Da Coconut but did not know how to make it. I asked a fellow captain and he simply told me "throw a couple limes in the blender with rum and Coco Lopez (the best brand of crème of coconut)". As you might expect, I was dubious to these instructions and wanted to try it out before serving it on a charter.

That is why I asked my good friend Steve to come over (he was anchored next to me in Charlotte Amalie) to try and figure it out. He was game (of course he was, since it was free booze) and we did exactly as instructed. We filled the blender with ice, added a good helping of coconut rum, a quarter cup of Coco Lopez, and two whole limes. Bloomp, bloomp in they went. What we got was bitter and clumpy because of the rinds. Of course, that did not stop us, we simply pulled out the spaghetti colander, strained the pulp and rind out, and drank it up (hey you cannot waste good rum, right?).

Now we are feeling good, because we figured we were on the right path. This time we would peel the limes and toss them in that way. We also figured out two cups of coconut rum with the quarter cup of Coco Lopez was the correct measurement, so we did not overfill the blender pitcher. Away we went for our second experiment/pitcher. This time it tasted good. It was crisp and refreshing, but the clumps of pulp took away from the experience. Out came the colander again and after straining the pitcher we enjoyed 2-3 more cups each.

When we finished the second pitcher we knew we were on to something, but we had to tweak it a little more. For the third pitcher we did everything the same except I juiced the two limes instead. Ahh, sweet success! This pitcher went down nice and smooth and we were feeling good....really good.....I mean REALLY, REALLY good. This probably had more to do with the fact that within an hour's time we shared three pitchers and had about a bottle and a half of coconut rum in us. Needless to say, he stumbled home (or the equivalent in a dinghy) and I went to bed.

The next evening, I called him over and said I want to make a pitcher just like we did the last time to make sure it was as good as we remembered and not just the rum in our blood. He, of course, said it was a good idea (free rum, remember) and in the name of customer service (to make sure it was perfect for guests) we made another pitcher in the blender. It was as good as remembered and is a refreshing drink on a hot afternoon.

Da Lime In Da Coconut	Bailey's Banana Colada	Bushwacker
2 cups Coconut rum	2 Bananas (peeled)	1/2 cup Bailey's
1/4 cup Coco Lopez	3/4 cup Banana rum	1/2 cup Kahlua
2 Limes (juiced)	1 1/4 cup Bailey's	1/2 cup Cream de coco
	1/4 cup Coco Lopez	1/2 cup Milk

All three of the above drinks need to be put into a blender 3/4 full of ice and will make about 5 drinks.

Mango Mojito	Hurricane	Goombay Smash
3 cups Mango rum	1 cup Rum	1 1/4 cup Dark rum
2 big spoons of sugar	1 cup Orange rum	3/4 cup Coconut rum
2cups Lemon juice	1 cup Pineapple rum	1 cup Pineapple rum
1 can Sprite	1 cup Orange juice	2 cup Pineapple juice
Fresh mint (crushed)	1 cup Pineapple juice	1/2 cup Lemon juice
	1/2 cup Grenadine	2 spoons of sugar
		Stir & pour then add dash of grenadine

These three drinks should be poured over ice in a glass. I have given the amounts in cups to be made in a pitcher for around 6 drinks, but if you want to make a single drink just convert to ounces instead and scale down.

STARTERS

- Appetizers
- Salads
- Soups

APPETIZERS

There was a time during one of my charter seasons when a boat named Sabbaticus sailed to St Thomas from points south of there in the Caribbean. I first met the family on Sabbaticus two years before in Annapolis, because I got bored and dinghied over to their boat and introduced myself. In Annapolis I spent a month hanging out with them and this time we spent the whole week hanging out along with the other crews they were sailing with at that time. We had such a great time spending the days playing volleyball on the beach and the nights playing billiards at the bar that it got me thinking about friendships and cruising.

In the cruising community, friendships take a different route than it does on land. For one you meet new people all the time on beaches, at sundowners, pot lucks, hiking, and multiple other opportunities. When you meet someone cruising you instantly have a common bond in your love of boats, cruising, and travel. So, it is quite easy to start conversations and connect with someone. I have been amazed at how quickly deep friendships form between cruisers. It is not uncommon to hang out with someone you just met for a week, a month, or even a year. Part of this is the connection you have with that person and part is the flexibility of the cruising lifestyle. If you meet crew on a boat that you enjoy and both of you are heading in the same general direction, then you might choose to buddy boat for a while and explore the area together. This can lead to them showing you somewhere you did not know about and vice versa. It also means you will know other people in the next anchorage, because they will be there. Sometimes while buddy boating you may choose to head somewhere due to picking up new crew or guests, getting repairs, resupplying, or you want to explore somewhere the other boat does not. That is ok because you can make plans to meet back up in a few days or weeks.

Eventually there will be a time that you will leave the company of another boat, whether that is after one day or one year, but there is always the possibility you will bump into each other in the future. It could be years from that moment and halfway around the world, but it is possible and happens more often than you might think. There are a dozen boats I regularly run into while cruising the Caribbean. Some are planned since we keep up with each other through social media and know where to look for each other, but others are happy coincidences. Like when some guests of mine bought a boat after being aboard the Guiding Light and dropped anchor next to me. What a surprise that was as they came over to show off their boat, Rondo. It was so wonderful to see them on their boat and getting into cruising. You could see the love for the lifestyle in their eyes along with the steep learning curve that comes in that first year of cruising.

I guess the moral of my rambling on is that friendships are quicker to form when you are on a boat and they can last a lifetime even if you don't see each other that often. With that said you never know who will end up stopping by and there is no better way to enjoy their company than with cocktails and appetizers as you watch the sun dip below the horizon. Don't worry though, there is always another day coming that will allow you to go out and meet even more new cruising friends. Happens every day about 12 hours after sunset.

BRUSCHETTA

- 2 tomatoes
- 1/2 onion
- 4 cloves of garlic
- 2 tsp oregano
- 2 Tbsp olive oil
- salt & pepper to taste
- 1 box of hardy crackers

-Chop tomatoes, onion, and garlic and put in a bowl.
-Add oregano, olive oil, salt, and pepper.
-Mix everything together and serve with crackers for dipping.

BUFFALO CHICKEN DIP

- 2 cans chicken
- 8 oz cream cheese (softened)
- 1/2 cup Frank's Red Hot Sauce
- 1/2 cup ranch dressing
- 1/2 cup bleu cheese (crumbled)
- 1/2 cup cheddar cheese (grated)
- 4 green onions (diced)
- 1 box of crackers or a package of celery & carrots

-Mix all ingredients together, except the green onions, and place into a baking dish.
-Bake at 350 degrees for 20 minutes.
-Garnish with green onions and serve with crackers or celery & carrot sticks.

CARIBBEAN LETTUCE WRAPS

- 1 lb lobster or crab meat
- 4 cups pineapple (chopped)
- 1 cucumber (chopped)
- 3 celery stalks (chopped)
- 1/2 red onion (chopped)
- 2 Tbsp orange juice
- 1 Tbsp lemon juice
- 1 Tbsp balsamic vinegar
- 1 Tbsp olive oil
- 1 Tbsp basil
- 1 Tbsp Dijon mustard
- salt & pepper to taste
- 1 head of lettuce (romaine or iceberg)

-Mix lobster, pineapple, cucumber, celery, and onion together.
-Mix orange juice, lemon juice, vinegar, oil, basil, and mustard in a bowl and whisk together.
-Pour mixture over meat and veggies and mix together.
-Spoon onto lettuce leaf and wrap.

STUFFED PEPPERS

- 6 peppers (any long, light green, mild variety will do)
- 2-3 Tbsp olive oil
- 8 oz feta cheese
- 1 Tbsp lemon juice
- 1/4 tsp pepper
- balsamic vinegar

-Remove stem and seeds of peppers and then butterfly them so they lay flat.
-Sauté peppers in the olive oil until starting to brown and blister.
-Mix feta cheese with the juice it came in, lemon juice, and pepper.
-Spoon mixture into each pepper and fold over.
-Drizzle balsamic vinegar over the top and serve.

SALADS

Sometimes you have adventures and other time you have misadventures. One misadventure I had at Rum Cay (Bahamas) started when I decided to take the dinghy outside the reef wall on the southern side of the island to see the HMS Conqueror. This 101-gun British ship of the line was only six years old when it was wrecked on the reef in 1861. The crew survived, but the ship was a total loss. Today the wooden hull is gone, but equipment is scattered all over a small area in about 30 feet of water and it is a great snorkel site. When I dove it, the waves were a foot or two tall but built to five feet as they passed over the reef. The waves hid the reef from my view and caused me to misalign the cut in the reef on my return. It happened so fast. One moment I was in 20 feet of water doing well and the second moment the wave picked me up and all I could see was the reef right in front of me. Unfortunately, there was nothing I could do as the wave brought the dinghy down on top of the reef and bounced me across it until I was back on the inside of the reef.

I checked out the damage and was happy that the top of the reef was all dead coral and the dinghy seemed to weather the trip intact and did not follow the Conqueror's fate. Since everything seemed ok I continued exploring and went to check out a huge salt pond. As I approached the entrance I noticed the dinghy was getting sluggish and by the time I got to the creek-like entrance I had zero thrust. I pulled the dinghy ashore and realized the prop had spun, or broken away from the hub, and was useless. It is designed to do this in order to protect the engine's lower unit but left me stranded two miles from town and my boat. My only course of action was to wade through the waist deep salt pond all the way back, so I could get another dinghy and tow mine back to the anchorage. The good news is that I got to explore the salt pond even better than I wanted. Haha.

Another misadventure I had at Rum Cay was a few days later when I chose to explore Flamingo Bay on the northwest part of the island. When you go there you have to maneuver through a maze of coral heads in Flamingo Bay and with good light it is not a problem. I was told by a local that Hartford Cave sits a couple miles from the bay and has lots of Lucayan petroglyphs. Since the new prop I ordered was a week away I used my kayak, and everything was going great paddling along the open north coast. That was, of course, until I tried to beach the kayak in a five-foot surf. I figured I would paddle hard and ride the wave in like a surfer and slide into the beach all cool like. The reality is that the wave picked up the kayak and tilted it forward until it seemed to be totally vertical. I panicked, jumped from the kayak, got tumbled in the surf, and plopped on the beach like a dead fish. I was fine but had to gather my equipment from all over the beach. After checking out the very cool petroglyphs I attempted to launch the kayak, which was not successful, as time after time, the waves turned the kayak and rolled it over in the surf. After three or four attempts, I finally figured out I had to swim the kayak out past the surf line and then climb in.

Misadventures like these make you look forward to the end of the day, so you can simply have dinner and relax and a salad is a great way to get dinner started.

MANGO, APPLE, & RADISH SALAD

- 10-15 radishes (sliced thin)
- 1 granny smith apple (peeled, cored, and sliced thin)
- 2 celery sticks (sliced thin)
- 1 mango (cubed)
- 1/2 cup sour cream
- 3 Tbsp Worcestershire sauce
- 1 Tbsp dill
- Salt & pepper

-Add radishes, apple, celery, and mango in bowl.
-Mix sour cream, Worcestershire sauce, dill, salt, and pepper in bowl.
-Add dressing to salad and toss to coat everything, but don't break up the mango.

CARROT PINEAPPLE SLAW

- 1 lb carrots (grated)
- 1 small can pineapple bits
- 1/2 cup peanuts (slightly crushed)
- 2 limes (juiced)
- 2 Tbsp olive oil
- Salt & pepper
- 1 Tbsp cilantro

-Combine all ingredients except cilantro and mix.
-Sprinkle cilantro on top and serve.

RADICCIO & FETA COUSCOUS

- 1 1/4 cups pearl couscous
- 1/2 head of radicchio (chopped)
- 8 oz feta cheese (crumbled)
- 1/3 cup olive oil
- 2 Tbsp white wine vinegar
- 1 lemon (juiced)
- salt & pepper

-Cook couscous as directed and drain.
-Combine rest of the ingredients.
-Let couscous cool a little bit and then mix with other ingredients.
-Chill before serving

PESTO SALAD

- 1 Tbsp pesto
- 1 carton cherry or grape tomatoes
- 8 oz mozzarella cheese
- 1 jar kalamata olives

-Cut tomatoes in half or quarters depending on size.
-Pit and cut olives in half.
-Chop mozzarella cheese into small chunks.
-Place everything in a bowl and mix together.

SOUPS

One year my Anegada Passage continued to be delayed. First, I had to rebuild my dinghy engine. Next, deal with some leaking hoses on the main engines. Finally, due to weather. It just kept blowing and blowing and blowing. The last good weather window to cross the Anegada Passage was the day I was rebuilding my dinghy engine.

Finally, the weather looked ok to cross. I was looking for 15 knots from the east or north of east with 3-5-foot swells. I got three different weather reports that all had the winds between 13-18 from 80-100 degrees with 4-6-foot waves, so I headed out from the North Sound on Virgin Gorda in the BVI.

I aimed for Nevis which is 125 miles away and I made it in 24 hours averaging five knots, but it wore me out and kicked my butt. The problem was the wind actually came from about 120 degrees, which meant I had to motor sail on one engine to make it and even then, the waves were almost straight ahead.

The first 80 miles is the actual Anegada Passage and then you come to Saba. I aimed perfectly, because I passed to the west only three miles from the island and halfway between the island and the Saba Bank (The Saba Bank is a 30-mile-wide shoal that is sometimes nasty, and you do not want to get on it). When I am sailing somewhere by myself I like to keep giving myself benchmarks. For example, 40-mile mark means I am half way across the Anegada Passage, 60 miles means I am halfway done, etc.

I started with a reef already tucked into the sail, but once night time came I went ahead and tucked a second one in. Good thing, because there were a couple thunderstorms that gave out 30 knot gusts. During one of them my bow navigation light got ripped off with a wave and was hanging by the wire. Why does this crap always happen at night when it is nasty out? Since I was by myself I stopped and thought through everything I was going to do and then I went forward with my tether to clip onto the boat and a roll of duct tape. Within 5 minutes I had the light taped into place. It looked Red Neck as heck, but it worked until I could fix it when I got to Nevis. God bless duct tape!

By the time I arrived at Nevis it was 8am and I had been up for over 24 hours and getting my butt kicked by the waves and gusts. I fell right to sleep for a couple hours and then got up and fixed several things including the navigation light before setting sail to the southwest corner of Guadeloupe. I have to admit I was not looking forward to this 85-mile sail after the last sail, but I had to get it out of the way. This is where 10 degrees can make a difference. The weather was the exact same, but my route was 10 degrees further south, which meant I could sail it. Granted it was still a close haul, but I was sailing it none the less and for the first 75% of the trip I was averaging over 8 knots and loving it the whole time. Then I got into the lee of Guadeloupe and it was like someone turned off the wind and waves! I was still 13 miles west of the island and 20 or so from my destination and the winds went from 20+ to 10 or less and really variable. After dorking around with the sails and angles I finally gave up and turned on one engine to motor sail the rest of the way.

I dropped anchor by 6pm and averaged 6 knots (being in the lee really knocked the average down). Regardless, as much as I hated the Anegada Passage, I loved the second day and it was all due to that 10-degree difference in the angle I was sailing. Now it is time to make some delicious warm soup and relax with a movie to recoup after two days of hard sailing.

LEMON, ARTICHOKE, CHICKEN SOUP

- 1 medium onion (diced)
- 1 Tbsp olive oil
- 1 can chicken (large)
- 1 can artichokes (bite size pieces)
- 4 cups chicken broth
- 2 lemons (sliced into wheels)
- 1/2 tsp chipotle powder
- 1 Tbsp thyme

-Sauté onion in olive oil until soften.
-Add everything else and let it simmer for 20-30 minutes.
-Serve with lemon wheels in soup, but don't eat the rind.

COCONUT, LIME, CHICKEN SOUP

- 2 large cans of chicken
- 2 cups water
- 1 can coconut milk
- 3 carrots (sliced thin and at an angle)
- 1/4 cup lime juice
- 1 Tbsp soy sauce
- 2 tsp curry

-Combine chicken, water, coconut milk, and carrots in a stock pot and boil until carrots are softened.
-Add lime juice, soy sauce, and curry and let it simmer for 5-10 minutes

FRENCH ONION SOUP

- 3 Tbsp butter
- 5 large onions (sliced thin)
- 1 Tbsp garlic (minced)
- 1 tsp sugar
- 1 tsp thyme
- 2 Tbsp flour
- 1/2 cup white wine
- 8 cups beef broth
- 1 loaf French bread
- 12 oz Swiss cheese (grated)

-Sauté onions with the butter in a large stock pot until they soften and start to brown.
-Add garlic, sugar, and thyme while continuing to cook until onions brown.
-Stir in flour and then wine and broth.
-Let simmer for 20 minutes.
-Slice bread into thick pieces and toast in oven.
-Ladle soup onto piece of bread and sprinkle grated cheese on top.

TOMATO & ROASTED PEPPER SOUP

- 2 Tbsp butter
- 2 Tbsp flour
- 1 can tomato juice (12 oz)
- 1 cup whipping cream
- 3 cans diced tomatoes (14 oz each)
- 1 jar roasted red peppers (diced)
- 1 tsp garlic (minced)
- 1 tsp sugar
- 1/2 tsp chipotle powder
- 1/2 cup sour cream

-In stock pot add butter and flour and stir until mixed.
-Add tomato juice and whipping cream and stir until smooth.
-Add tomatoes, red peppers, garlic, sugar, and chipotle and simmer for 15-20 minutes.
-Serve either chunky or blended smooth with a dollop of sour cream in the middle of soup.

SPINACH SOUP

- 2 Tbsp olive oil
- 1 onion (diced)
- 1 Tbsp thyme
- 2 potatoes (large)(cubed small to cook faster)
- 1 can coconut milk
- 4 cups chicken broth
- 5 cups spinach (or any similar leafy green)
- hot sauce
- ground pepper

-Sauté onion in olive oil until tender then add thyme, potatoes, coconut milk, and broth.
-Simmer until potatoes are soft and done.
-Add spinach and simmer about five more minutes.
-Mix in a blender until soup is smooth.
-Pour soup into bowls and sprinkle with pepper and put a squirt of hot sauce in the middle of the soup.

MAIN COURSES

- Beef
- Chicken
- Pork
- Seafood
- Vegetarian

BEEF

My favorite guests aboard the Guiding Light has been my parents and I have lots of fun stories from their visits.

The first one is when I needed to clean up some water in the back hold. I went into the hatch head first up to my waist, so I could reach the bottom with a sponge. Everything was ok until I tried to get out and realized a bar across my back had gotten behind my shoulder blades. I could not free myself and had gotten myself stuck like Winnie the Pooh in the rabbit's hole (my mother's words when she saw my butt sticking out of the hatch). With her help I finally got out and deserved my dad's teasing. Haha

This trip was the end of a rough four years for my dad due to multiple heart surgeries and now he gets winded easily and moves slower than he used to. With that said we took the dinghy out to go snorkeling, but sadly he only lasted 2 minutes before he was DONE!!! He was not near the dinghy, but that did not stop him from getting out of the water. He simply climbed a sea urchin infested rock like a kid playing king of the hill. Once I finally got him back into the dinghy he noticed he had five urchin wounds, but he felt lucky he did not get one right in the butt.

I did learn two things with them onboard. First, old people love to know what the weather is and check it every morning. The first day they announced it was 60 degrees and drizzly, which confused me since it never gets to 60 in the Caribbean until they rattled off the weather in 35 different locations across the country. Whereas I only care about the weather where I am, they want to know what it is like where everyone else is, including the burial site of a childhood dog!

The other thing I learned was old people have to retire, because all their time is taken up with doctors' visits and taking pills. There were times during our sail they had to restock the pill dispensers. It seemed like this activity brought joy to their lives and a twinkle to my dad's eyes. They would bring up a suitcase load of bottles and plunk one pill in each bin. I warned them ahead of their flight home, if the DEA stopped them thinking they were drug traffickers, I was going to let them to rot in a Puerto Rican jail. Haha.

The final story was due to the fact I was hauling the boat out at the end of our cruise and we were trying to get rid of the food I had aboard. Towards the very end my mom made what we called "clean out the cabinet" casserole. She used rice, taco mix, carrots, celery, and other stuff and came up with a pretty tasty meal with lots of leftovers. The next night when she pulled it out and plopped it on my plate I stared at it and all I could see was a pile of dog food. I stated as much, and my dad jumped on this and to my mother's dismay her "clean out the cabinet" casserole was instantaneously renamed "Dog Food"! Luckily, I have several other tasty beef dishes!!!!!!

CARIBBEAN MEATBALLS

- 1 mango (cubed)
- 1 papaya (cubed)
- 2 Tbsp plain yogurt
- 1/2 tsp paprika
- 1/4 tsp chipotle
- 1 1/2 cups rice (white)
- 1 can coconut milk
- 1 1/2 cups chicken broth
- 1 Lb chorizo
- 1 Lb ground beef
- 3/4 cup seasoned bread crumbs
- 1/2 cup green onion (diced)
- 1/2 cup tamarind juice
- 1/2 cup lime juice
- 1/2 cup brown sugar
- 1/4 cup ketchup

-Put mango, papaya, yogurt, paprika, and chipotle in a blender and puree. Set aside.
-Bring rice, coconut milk, and broth to a boil and then simmer until it is done. Set aside.
-Mix the chorizo, ground beef, bread crumbs, and half the green onions together and then make into meatballs. Set aside.
-In a saucepan bring tamarind juice, lime juice, brown sugar, and ketchup to a boil. Add the meatballs and cook fully by rotating and coating with the liquid.
-On each plate spread some of the fruit puree around. Top with a helping of rice, then place some meatballs on top of the rice, and sprinkle remaining onion on top.

LEMON PEPPER FLANK STEAK

- 2 lb flank steak
- 1/4 cup lemon pepper spice
- 2 Tbsp olive oil
- 1 package frozen spinach
- 1 can mushrooms
- 4 oz mozzarella cheese (grated)

-Coat the steak with the oil and generously sprinkle lemon pepper all over steak. Repeat on other side and let it stand for 10 minutes.
-Warm up spinach and mushrooms (save a few for garnish) in a sauce pan.
-Put spinach, mushrooms, and cheese at one end of the steak and roll it into a log.
-Put the rolled steak in a loaf pan, sprinkle the top with more lemon pepper, and add mushroom garnish to the top.
-Bake for one hour at 375 degrees.

GINGERED SNOW PEAS & SIRLOIN STRIPS

- 4 Tbsp olive oil
- 1/4 cup fresh ginger (cut into matchsticks)
- 1 lb snow peas
- 4 green onions (diced)
- 1 red pepper (cut into strips)
- 1/2 cup chicken broth
- 2 Tbsp soy sauce
- 1 tsp Chinese chili-garlic sauce
- 1 tsp crushed garlic
- 1 1/2 lbs of fajita strips of beef
- 2 Tbsp balsamic vinegar
- parmesan cheese (grated)

-Use half the oil and sauté the ginger until softened (1 minute).
-Add snow peas and sauté until tender and ginger browns (2 minutes).
-Stir in red pepper, onion, broth, soy sauce, and chili-garlic.
-Once mixed well and thickened a little pour everything into a bowl and keep warm.
-Heat rest of the oil with garlic on high heat and sauté beef strips until starting to brown.
-Add the vinegar and cook just until no pink is left.
-Place beef into bowls, top with the snow peas, grate cheese over bowls, and serve.

PEPPERCORN STEAK

- 6 Tbsp black peppercorn
- 6 steaks (1/2 lb each)
- 3 Tbsp butter
- 1 Tbsp vegetable oil
- 4 Tbsp brandy
- 1 cup heavy cream
- 1 tsp garlic (minced)

-Crack the peppercorn coarsely.
-Press the peppercorn into both sides of the steaks, coating them completely.
-Melt the butter with the oil in a frying pan over medium high heat and add the steaks.
-Cook to desired doneness and then stack on a plate and place in a warmed oven.
-Add the brandy to the pan to deglaze it. Let it reduce to half while scrapping the pan.
-Add the cream and garlic and boil while stirring until the mixture has reduced by a third.
-Plate the steaks, pour sauce over each one, and serve.

POMEGRANATE CHIMICHURRI

- 6 Steaks
- salt & pepper
- 6 Tbsp olive oil
- 1 cup pomegranate seeds
- 3 Tbsp balsamic vinegar
- 4 Tbsp fresh parsley (chopped finely)
- 4 Tbsp fresh cilantro (chopped finely)
- 2 Tbsp fresh mint (chopped finely)

-Season steaks with salt and pepper.
-In skillet, heat 2 Tbsp oil over high and cook steaks until desired doneness.
-Let the meat rest about 10 minutes before slicing to save juices.
-Mix remaining oil with rest of the ingredients and spoon over sliced steaks.

<u>RED WINE & ROSEMARY STEAKS</u>

- 6 filet mignons
- salt
- 2 Tbsp olive oil
- 2 Tbsp butter
- 2 shallots (minced)
- 1/2 cup dry red wine
- 2 tsp brown sugar
- 1 Tbsp balsamic vinegar
- 1 tsp Dijon mustard
- 1/2 Tbsp rosemary

-Sprinkle both sides of steak with salt.
-Melt butter in oil and add steaks to sear on medium high heat to desire doneness.
-Stack steaks on a plate and place in a warmed oven to keep warm.
-Add shallots and sauté until soft.
-Add wine and reduce by half on high heat.
-Add sugar, vinegar, and mustard. Let it cook until it thickens.
-Stir in rosemary and sauté for a minute or so.
-Place steaks in the sauce to coat them, flip, and then plate. Spoon sauce over each one.

CHICKEN

It is usually a good thing when a beautiful woman knocks on my hull, but this story is the exception. You see one particular Thursday morning at 1am a squall passed through making the wind really to pick up and start raining hard. I was almost asleep when I felt the boat bump something. I rushed up and saw a boat was in front of me. I mean RIGHT in front of me. In fact, one hull was between my bows. YIKES!!!!!

I put on my foul weather jacket and ran to the bow just as a beautiful lady was coming out to the back of her boat. She was panicking and did not know what to do since her boyfriend/captain was back in the States for a week. I told her she probably dragged anchor and she needed to get the engines started and re-anchor.

She ran around to do something and came back out saying the boat would not move. At this point she basically begged me to take control of her boat and tell her what to do. I told her we need to get the engines running and pull in some of the anchor chain. She went here and there flipping switches but could not understand why the engine gauges did not register even though we could hear one running. All the while she kept pushing a button saying it wouldn't start. As calmly as I could I told her she was pushing the stop button and the ignition key had not been moved to the on position. With that fixed, one engine registered and I started the other one. She then explained the throttle had to be turned on, which she did.

I then asked where the anchor controls were, so we could start bringing it in, but her bridle was snagged. I asked for a piece of line and tied it off ahead of the bridle and pulled tight to a cleat. I told her to let some chain out and then I had to tell her to push the button the OTHER way. With the bridle under no stress I was able to get it off, untie the line, and she started bringing it in. She got to where the anchor chain is marked and told me we were at the red mark. I said great, but how much chain does the red mark mean she has out? She did not know just that they almost always go to the red mark.

I suggested she move the boat to the dock and re-anchor in the morning. She told me whatever I thought was best and pulled out dock lines and fenders. We got the boat ready and I asked if she wanted to drive the boat, but she graciously offered to let me. Surprise, surprise.

The boat has an interior helm with an exterior steering station outside, which means I could not see well enough inside and there were no instruments outside. So here I was driving a 55-foot cat I had never been on before, with a steering station at the mast (I am used to being much further back), without instruments, going to a dock I have never approached, and in the dark. I was a bit nervous, but I got the boat along the dock and we got it tied up. Now I don't have to worry about it dragging anchor again tonight.

This entire time she was wearing a foul weather jacket and kept holding it closed. Of course, I was so focused on protecting our boats I did not notice and just thought she was cold. It was not until we finished securing the boat to the dock that I noticed under the jacket she was only wearing a tank top and panties and right then she rushed down stairs to put shorts on. Like I said, it is usually a good thing when a beautiful chick knocks on your boat, but only if you get to enjoy their company.....and their choice of attire. I guess I have to settle with a good chicken dish.

ASPARAGUS LEMON CHICKEN

- 1 1/2 lbs small purple potatoes (quartered)
- 4 Tbsp butter
- salt & pepper (to taste)
- 2 lbs chicken
- 1 bundle of asparagus
- 2 lemons (cut into wheels)
- 2 Tbsp thyme

-Sauté potatoes in half the butter until they are golden.
-Place potatoes in a 9x13 pan with chicken on top of them. Season chicken with salt and pepper and bake for 20 minutes in 350-degree oven.
-Put asparagus, lemons, remaining butter, and thyme on chicken and potatoes. Bake for another 15 minutes until asparagus is tender and chicken is done.
-When serving use the pan juice to drizzle on each serving.

BBQ JALAPENO CHICKEN

- 6 jalapenos (cleaned and diced)
- 6 oz cream cheese (softened)
- 12 oz colby-jack cheese (shredded)
- 6 chicken breasts
- 24 slices of bacon
- toothpicks
- 1 bottle of BBQ sauce

-Sauté jalapenos and mix with both cheeses once done.
-Butterfly chicken, put a spoonful of the cheese mixture on chicken, and roll up.
-Wrap four pieces of bacon around rolled up chicken and hold in place with toothpicks.
-Grill for 5 minutes and give a quarter turn and then repeat 3 more time for a total of 20 minutes grilling time, basting with BBQ sauce each turn.

ENCHILADAS

- 2 lbs chicken (or 2 cans chicken)
- 1 package of cream cheese (softened)
- 10 corn tortillas (warmed)
- 3 cans of red enchilada sauce
- 16 oz cheddar cheese (shredded)

-If using fresh chicken cut into strips and cook in oven until done.
-Divide cream cheese into 10 servings and smear onto each tortilla.
-Put 1/10 of the chicken onto each tortilla, roll up, and place in a 9x13 pan.
-Cover the rolled tortillas with the enchilada sauce and then the cheese.
-Bake for 20 minutes at 350 degrees so the cheese melts.

SPINACH FLORENTINE CREPES

- 1 chicken breast (diced)
- 1 tsp garlic (minced)
- 1 Tbsp butter
- 10 oz cream of chicken soup
- 1/4 cup milk
- 3 oz Swiss cheese (shredded)
- 1 package frozen spinach
- 10 crepes (see breakfast section for recipe)
- hollandaise sauce
- 2 egg yolks
- 2 Tbsp lemon juice
- 1 stick of butter (cold)

-Sauté chicken and garlic in butter until brown.

-Pour in milk and soup. Simmer until thickened a bit.

-Add spinach and cheese and stir until cheese is melted and mixture is reduced.

-Make hollandaise sauce by combining egg yolks and lemon juice in a small sauce pan and put over very low heat. Add stick of butter and stir continually until butter is melted. If sauce curdles, add 1 Tbsp water and stir until smooth.

-Place 1/2 cup of chicken sauce on each crepe and wrap. Top with hollandaise sauce.

GREEK ROASTED CHICKEN

- 8 chicken breasts
- 1 Tbsp olive oil
- 1 Tbsp oregano
- salt & pepper (to taste)
- 1 can tomato sauce
- 1 jar kalamata olives (pitted and halved)
- 1 cup feta cheese (crumbled)

-Heat oil in a skillet and brown chicken on both sides (this will only sear it).
-Place chicken in a 9x13 pan and sprinkle them with the oregano, salt, and pepper.
-Pour the tomato sauce over the chicken and put olives on top of this.
-Bake for 15 minutes at 375 degrees.
-Sprinkle feta over chicken and bake another 15 minutes or until chicken is done.

TEQUILA LIME CHICKEN

- 8 chicken breasts

Marinade
- 1 cup water
- 1 lime juiced
- 1 tsp tequila
- 1/3 cup teriyaki sauce
- 2 tsp garlic (minced)
- 1/2 tsp salt
- 1 tsp ginger (powder)

Mexi-dressing
- 1/4 cup mayonnaise
- 1/4 cup sour cream
- 2 Tbsp milk
- 1 small tomato (finely diced)
- 1 tsp balsamic vinegar
- 1 tsp hot sauce
- 1 tsp dill
- 1/2 tsp paprika
- 1/2 tsp cumin

- 1 cup cheddar/monterrey jack cheese (finely shredded)
- chips (Tostitos Lime if possible, but Pringles Jalapeno work also)

-Make marinade and soak chicken in it for 2-3 hours in the frig.
-Mix up the mexi-dressing and chill.
-Grill chicken for 10 minutes per side or until done.
- Spoon mexi-dressing on chicken and top with shredded cheese. Grill until cheese melts.
-Place a chicken breast onto a bed of crumbled chips.

PORK

I get asked how I chose to move onto a boat and what it took to accomplish the task. The first part is quite simple. My life changed due to a decision made by another person, so I had a decision of my own to make. Do I stay in Golden, CO where I have been happy for 18 years playing soccer and volunteering for the fire department or do I embrace this change and do something I talked about doing someday when I retired? There were 13 or so things that lined up at this exact time in my life, some good and some bad, leading me to believe God was telling me that if I want to go cruising on a boat now is the time to do it.

Once I decided this was the course of action for me I embraced the idea of downsizing and had a fantastic two weeks selling off almost all my stuff until I had it down to a car load and a desk I wanted to keep. During this time, I did some work on my house for a month and then placed it up for sell on December 22, 2008. You must remember this is right in the middle of the financial meltdown, but my house had an offer in less time than it took me to drive 14 hours to my parents for Christmas. Everything went smoothly and was just another example that this was the right course for me.

The weekend after I closed on the house my best friend and I met in Ft Lauderdale to look at boats. We knew a catamaran was the right style but had no clue about the different models out there. So, we spent a long weekend driving four hours south to Key West and four hours north to Dayton Beach looking at 8-10 different models of catamarans. I was amazed that I could not stand up properly in the galley in many of the models. My boat broker almost got fired when he said "is that a big deal? How often are you going to need to stand in the galley?" I was thinking "really? I am going to go with three times a day!" At the end of the weekend the only models that worked for me within my budget were the Lagoon 380 & 410 and a Leopard 42. Of the three I went with the Lagoon 410 because I felt it gave me the most bang for the buck and I am so happy I made that decision.

Now that I found the model I wanted, finding the actual boat was way easier. I simply chose the first Lagoon 410 I saw on my broker's website. To this day I still think I got a great boat at a great price. Later I found out that I was buying Brio (their name for the boat) from some friends of a family friend. Small world!!!

You would think all of the above was the hard part, but it all seemed to flow together perfectly. The rest of the story is where the wrinkles came. First was trying to find insurance for a boat I was buying in a foreign country, sailing across the Caribbean Sea and Gulf of Mexico for two weeks, and keeping south of Houston, TX the first year, which is in the hurricane zone. Everyone I talked to was ok with one or two of these circumstances, but not all three. I finally found a company that said no problem. The other issue I had was getting a mortgage. My mortgage broker told me it would have been better if I still owned my house, because the financial meltdown made lending tight and companies wanted to see collateral. I told her the boat could be collateral, but she said, "they would prefer collateral that you cannot simply sail away on and they will never see again." The only thing I could respond with was "fair enough, but what is done is done and I have already sold my house. Nothing I can do about it now." In the end she was able to secure a mortgage for a little over half the boat and I had to bring home the BACON for the rest. Do you notice how I brought it around and tied it to the pork recipes? Haha.

ASIAN BBQ PORK CHOPS

- 6 pork chops
- 1 Tbsp olive oil
- 1 1/2 Tbsp fish sauce
- 1 tsp soy sauce
- 1 tsp sugar
- 1/4 tsp pepper
- 1/2 tsp curry
- 2 tsp garlic (minced)
- 1/2 tsp cilantro (minced)
- 3 Tbsp coconut milk

-Mix all of the ingredients, except the pork, together to form a marinade.
-Set aside a small portion of the marinade to use for basting during grilling.
-Marinate the pork chops for at least 2 hours in the remaining marinade.
-Grill the pork chops and coat with the basting marinate as needed.

DIJON PORK CHOPS

- 6 pork chops
- 1 tsp pepper
- 3 tsp rosemary
- 3 Tbsp garlic
- 6 Tbsp Dijon mustard
- 3 Tbsp lemon juice
- 2 Tbsp dry sherry
- 2 Tbsp soy sauce
- 4 Tbsp olive oil
- 1 tsp sage

-Press pepper, garlic, and rosemary into pork chops and then coat with the Dijon. Repeat on other side.
-Mix lemon juice, sherry, soy sauce, olive oil, and sage.
-Let the pork chops marinate in mixture for at least three hours.
-Grill pork chops until desired doneness is achieved.

EGGPLANT RICOTTA

- 1 eggplant
- 8 oz prosciutto or ham
- 1 cup ricotta cheese
- 1 jar marina sauce
- 8 oz mozzarella (shredded)

-In a 13x9 pan layer sliced eggplant, ricotta cheese, prosciutto, marina sauce, and repeat.
-Sprinkle mozzarella cheese on top.
-Bake for 30 minutes at 350 degrees.

PORK CHOPS WITH PAPAYA SALSA

- 6 pork chops

Glaze

- 2 Tbsp water
- 2 Tbsp syrup
- 1 tsp chipotle

Salsa

- 1 cup papaya (chopped fine)
- 2 Tbsp red onion (minced)
- 2 jalapenos (minced)
- 1.5 Tbsp cilantro
- juice from half a lime
- 2 tsp syrup

-Grill pork chops and coat with glaze each time you flip them.
-Mix all salsa ingredients and put on top of cooked pork chops.

RASPBERRY JALAPENO PORK

- 1/2 stick of butter
- 4 jalapenos (seeded and diced finely)
- 2 cups frozen raspberries
- 1 granny smith apple (cored, peeled, and diced finely)
- 1 Tbsp brown sugar
- 6 pork chops
- salt

-Sauté jalapenos in butter, then add raspberries & apple, and let simmer for 6-8 minutes.
-Add sugar and simmer for another 10-15 minutes.
-Sprinkle salt on both sides of pork chops and grill to desired doneness.
-Spoon raspberry sauce over pork chops.

SEAFOOD

A couple years ago I was in The Bight at Norman Island with a family that had three teenage kids of 18, 16, and 14. At about 10pm we returned to the Guiding Light after having dinner and drinks on the Willy T, which is a famous floating bar that used to be a ship. In the British Virgin Islands, the Willy T has the reputation of being the rowdiest bar and I have seen everything here over the years, and I mean EVERYTHING!!!!!! Anyway, my guests and I were doing my favorite activity on the Willy T and that is having a blast jumping off the second floor of the boat/bar into the 30-40 feet deep water. At night it is even more exciting because everything is dark, and you do not know what is down there.

So, with all the jumping and diving we did at the Willy T you would think we were worn out, but as I was pulling the dinghy up I took advantage of where the dad was standing and pushed him into the water. This set off another half hour of jumping, pushing, and enjoying the water off the back of the Guiding Light, but finally we all got out and started drying off and settling in.

Not more than 10 minutes after getting out of the water we hear some large splashes out in the darkness. Given the reputation the Willy T has I assumed it was a drunk idiot swimming or paddle boarding at night. I grab my flashlight to make sure whoever this idiot was they were ok and safe. As soon as I shined the light out across the water a three-foot tarpon swam towards the boat and quickly went under it. Seeing a tarpon at night is quite common and they can get up to six feet long. What was unusual was the speed at which he was swimming. Tarpon usually just hang out under the boat waiting for scrap food to be thrown overboard.

I tried to get everyone to come see the fish swimming, since everyone loves to watch the fish under the boat....especially at night. But before I can even get the whole sentence out of my mouth we saw a seven-foot great hammerhead shark chasing the tarpon. No wonder that first sucker was booking it so fast for the boat. The hammerhead came so close to the boat that he would have hit his head on the swim ladder if I still had it down. Both the tarpon and shark made a second loop and bolted under the boat again and that was the last we saw or heard of them. I don't even know if the tarpon survived to swim another day.

The whole experience only lasted five seconds or so, but it left a lasting impression on those kids because they keep saying "we were just in that water" and "what if we were in there when they came by?" In the end I got that shark back for scaring my guest, because the next night I served a seafood dinner that had them raving about the wonders coming out of the ocean. □

GUATEMALAN STYLE FISH

- 6 fish fillets (firm white fish like mackerel or tilapia is best)
- 1 lime
- 1/2 onion (grated)
- 1 Tbsp garlic (minced)
- 1 tsp chipotle powder
- 1 tsp oregano
- 1 tsp cilantro
- 1 tsp pepper
- 3 Tbsp olive oil
- 1/2 cup flour

-Squeeze lime juice on fillets and then rub onion and garlic on both sides.
-Sprinkle fillets with each seasoning on both sides and let sit for 15 minutes to marinate.
-Heat oil in a pan until it is very hot.
-Coat each fillet with flour, knock off excess, and fry in oil until crispy.

LEMON GINGER SALMON

- 8 salmon steaks
- 1/4 cup butter
- 3 lemons
- 2 Tbsp ginger (grated)
- 1 Tbsp sugar
- 1 bag spinach
- salt & pepper

-Thinly slice one lemon, grate the rind on one of the remaining two lemons, and juice both. Add sugar and ginger and set aside.
-Sauté spinach in a bit of water until it wilts.
-Sauté salmon in butter and once flipped add lemon juice and rind mixture.
-When done place over spinach and continue sautéing lemon sauce adding sliced lemons.
-Spoon sauce and lemons over fish.

MANGO, FETA, FISH TACOS

- 2 1/2 lbs mahi mahi
- 1 jar salsa
- 1 mango (chopped)
- 1 cup guacamole
- 1/2 cup chopped tomatoes
- 12 flour tortillas
- 8 oz feta cheese (crumbled)

-Cook fish in a skillet with olive oil.
-Shred fish and mix with salsa.
-Combine mango, guacamole, and tomatoes.
-Spoon fish mixture onto tortillas, top with mango guacamole, and sprinkle with feta.

MANGO PASTA

- 1 lb pasta
- 2 mangos (very ripe)
- 1 cucumber (diced)
- 1 red pepper (diced)
- 1 red onion (diced)
- 1 lime
- 1-2 tsp chipotle powder (to taste)
- 2 tsp salt
- 1 lb shrimp (uncooked)
- 1 jar sweet chili sauce

-Prepare pasta as directed.
-Mash mango until it forms a sauce.
-Add cucumber, red pepper, red onion, and juice of lime. Mix all together.
-Mix in chipotle powder, salt, and cilantro to the mixture.
-Sauté shrimp in sweet chili sauce until done.
-Spoon on veggie sauce on top of pasta and place shrimp on the side.

PROSCIUTTO & SAGE FISH

- 6 white, firm fish fillets
- 2 tsp pepper
- 2 Tbsp sage
- 12 slices prosciutto
- 1/4 cup flour
- olive oil
- 1/3 cup white wine
- 2 Tbsp butter

-Season each fish with pepper and sage and then wrap with two slices of prosciutto each.
-Dust the fish with flour and pat off extra.
-Fry in a skillet in olive oil until done.
-Plate the fish and pour the wine into the pan and let it reduce before adding the butter.
-Spoon this mixture over the fish and serve.

TUNA STEAKS TOPPED WITH GINGER & CARROT SALAD

- 6 tuna steaks
- 3 Tbsp olive oil
- 2 Tbsp soy sauce
- 1 lime (juiced)
- Salad
- 2 inch piece of ginger (peeled and grated)
- 1 carrot (grated)
- 2 Tbsp balsamic vinegar
- 1 Tbsp olive oil
- 1 Tbsp soy sauce
- 1 tsp sugar
- 2 Tbsp water
- Bread slices (toasted)
- Avocado slices

-Mix olive oil, soy sauce, and lime juice and marinate tuna steaks for at least 30 minutes.
-Mix all salad ingredients together and set aside.
-Sear tuna steaks in frying pan for 3-6 minutes per side depending on desired doneness.
-Lay bread on plate with tuna half on it, top with salad, and then avocado slices.

VEGETARIAN

Moving on to a boat from a life led 2000 miles inland can be a bit overwhelming. I arrived at the airport in the British Virgin Islands at 9pm the night I closed on the boat. The previous owner was there to meet me as we walked a couple hundred feet to dinghy to my new boat. Talk about a change, walking from an international airport less than two football fields and being on a beach.

I spent the entire next day being overwhelmed with information as I tried to absorb everything Paul was telling me about the boat. Imagine buying a house and having to learn how the toilets flush, the gas gets to the oven, working the communications, and turning on the power to name a few. Then you must get boat specific stuff like the engines, making water, bilges, etc. Like I said, OVERWHELMING!

I even had to save my boat that first day when this idiot, who anchored too close the day before, wanted to leave. The problem was the boats shifted and his anchor was now under my boat. He kept trying to get it up as he inched closer and closer to the Guiding Light and would have hit me if we did not have fenders out and ready to put between the boats. Luckily there was a great couple who squeezed their inflatable in between the boats to act as a giant fender.

Whether all the information was absorbed or not, Paul left the next morning at 5am. I told him to take the dinghy, leave it at the dock, and I would flag someone down to bum a ride to it later. I was finally alone on my own boat. Yes!!! I spent the day going through all the cabinets, lockers, bilges, and other hidey holes to see what all was in my boat. It was like a treasure hunt.

A couple days later I had a friend join me and we hung out in the BVI for over two more weeks getting the boat organized and ready to sail it to the Houston, TX area. Several days before our planned sail to the USA another crew member joined us. Mark had just lost his wife to brain cancer three weeks prior and days before she passed away she asked him to spread her ashes at the Bitter End in the BVI due to an incredible vacation they had there in the past. At the time he did not know when he would be able to do so, but he promised her. A week later he met my friend, through her neighbor, and he joined the crew. The first place we went was the Bitter End where he was able to grant her dying wish within weeks of her asking and her ashes were scattered in the place that she called "her favorite place on earth". Did God put him in the right place at the right time to join us or what?

Three weeks after taking ownership of the Guiding Light I had a crew ready to help me sail it 2000 miles to Houston. None of us had any blue water experience, but the weather report looked good and as I always say, "experience is the thing you get right after you needed it". The funny thing is that I had no clue where we were going to go in Houston, but I left the chore of finding dock space up to my best friend Joel. When we left we had 20 knots of wind and 6-7 foot waves from behind and we ended up sailing seven of the first eight days to Grand Cayman Island, where we stopped for 24 hours to get provisions, water, weather, and other supplies. The funny thing is the first four days all of us were a little seasick. I even contemplated if I made the wrong lifestyle change. Luckily it passed, and we were all loving life from day 5 on. Once we left Grand Cayman we proceeded to have zero wind across the Gulf of Mexico and motored seven of the eight days to Houston. By the time we reached Houston and navigated to the dock Joel found, we had been at sea for 16 days. We were more than ready for dry land, a hot shower, and some fresh veggies.

BALSAMIC PEAR PASTA

- Pasta (ravioli is best)
- 2 Tbsp olive oil
- 1/4 cup almonds (slivered)
- 1 1/2 sticks of butter
- 1 pear (cubed)
- 1 tsp basil
- salt & pepper
- balsamic vinegar (drizzled)

-Cook pasta
-Sauté almonds in oil and put aside.
-Melt and cook butter until brown and then add pear to stop butter from cooking.
-Lower heat and add basil and almonds to mixture and salt & pepper to taste.
-Spoon over pasta and drizzle a bit of balsamic vinegar over the top and serve.

SIDE DISHES

Bread is not something most of us think too much about. We simply go to the store and pick the right one for our needs from a selection presented to us along an entire wall or row. The biggest decision we make is white or wheat, low cost or high end, maybe even fresh French bread from the bakery. Easy peasy.

This is the regard I had given to bread my entire life including when I started cruising. The first year I cruised the Gulf and East Coast of America and once every week or two I would stop by a grocery store to get more food, including bread. The next year I started cruising the Bahamas and had no problem finding bread in the capital of Nassau or the big towns of Freeport, Marsh Harbor, George Town, and Spanish Wells.

The problem started showing itself as I cruised the out islands that were either not populated or had small villages with less than 300 people. Here I started finding packaged bread at increasing prices. $5, $6, $7, even $8 for a loaf of bread and the age was always in question. Sometimes you were paying these prices for bread made at home by a local.

Things changed when I made it to George Town at the southern end of the Exumas. For cruisers in the Bahamas this is the focus point that everyone wants to get to. At times there are 400 boats in the anchorage and dinghies are buzzing back and forth. It is always a hot bed of activity. Every morning there is a cruisier net on the VHF radio telling everyone all the scheduled activities going on that day, items for sale, get togethers, and so much more. It felt like I was at summer camp for adults. Everyone loved it and many of the cruisers came back every year and parked their boats right in the anchorage all winter.

One day while I was there, one of my friends decided to go to a cooking and recipe exchange gathering. She came back to our little group and told us what all she had learned. She even had a stack of recipes and asked if we wanted any. The French bread recipe caught my eye immediately. Now I could make bread myself and not pay the ransom the stores were asking for who know how old loaves of bread. I started right then and there making homemade bread and continued throughout the Bahamas. Every now and then I would change the technique to make it a little easier. First, I moved from placing the rolled out dough on a cookie sheet to placing them in loaf pans, so sandwiches were easier to make with the bread. Next the recipe called for pushing the rising bread down every ten minutes for over an hour. Who has time for that? There were other changes, but the actual recipe was never altered.

Life was good as I cruised the rest of the Bahamas, back to the US, back to the Bahamas, down to the Turks and Caicos, and then sailed to the Virgin Islands, all while having homemade bread aboard the boat.

Once I got to the Virgin Islands I started my charter business and was looking for ways to distinguish myself from all the other boats. That is when I decided to make my homemade bread to use for sandwiches at lunch time. This became a huge hit and I have become known as the bread captain by the brokers and other charter boats. In fact, many of the ladies, that are chefs on other charter boats, say I make them look bad. I find this funny since I know they are better cooks than me and they put out three hot meals and a midafternoon snack everyday of their charters, but just because I make homemade bread for my guests they are jealous. Let me tell you, that is quite a compliment!!!!!!

BALSAMIC ASPARAGUS

- 1 bundle of asparagus
- 3 Tbsp olive oil
- 1/2 tsp basil
- 1/2 tsp oregano
- 1/2 tsp rosemary
- 1/2 tsp sage
- 1/2 tsp thyme
- 2 tsp balsamic vinegar

-Sauté asparagus in olive oil.
-While sautéing add each spice making sure all the asparagus is covered.
-Right before done add vinegar and sauté for half a minute to minute longer and then serve.

SWEET & SOUR BRUSSEL SPROUTS

- 1 package brussels sprouts
- 4 Jalapenos
- 1/2 jar guava jelly
- 3 Tbsp butter

-Sauté everything together and serve.

HOMEMADE BREAD

- 2 1/2 cup warm water
- 2 Tbsp yeast
- 1/4 cup sugar
- 2 tsp salt
- 2 Tbsp oil
- 6 cups flour

-Add everything except flour to a large bowl and use a whisk to stir well.
-Add 6 cups flour and stir everything together. Eventually you will have to mix by hand and fold it over several time to knead it.
-Divide and place into two greased loaf pans.
-Let it rise for 1 hour (sometimes more, should be raised over the top of the pan) and then bake for 30 minutes at 350 degrees.

-If you want you can add one of the following to the bread for different flavors:
- rosemary
- black pepper & onion
- 2 Tbsp cinnamon, 1/2 tsp nutmeg, & 1/2 tsp clove
- 4 oz sausage, onion, 1 cup monterey jack cheese
- bacon & cheddar
- olives, sundried tomatoes, & feta
- garlic & thyme

CARROTS IN GRAND MARNIER

- 6 carrots (sliced thin on an angle)
- 1/2 stick of butter
- 1 cup orange juice
- 2 tsp nutmeg
- 2 tsp cinnamon
- 1/4 cup sugar
- 2 oz Grand Marnier

-Boil carrots until softened.
-Mix butter, orange juice, nutmeg, cinnamon, and sugar in pan stirring so it will not stick.
-Add Grand Marnier and it will thicken immediately.
-Toss in drained carrots, mixing thoroughly, and serve.

RICE SIDES

Spring Herb Rice

- 1 cup rice
- 1 onion (chopped)
- 1 Tbsp olive oil
- 1 Tbsp butter
- 1 cup celery (sliced)
- 1 cup mushroom (sliced)
- 1/2 tsp salt
- 1/4 tsp pepper
- 2 Tbsp Italian herbs

-Put rice in boiling water, bring back to a boil, and then simmer for 15 minutes or until liquid is absorbed. Let rice stand covered for 5 minutes
-Sauté onion in olive oil and butter.
-Add celery, mushrooms, salt, and pepper.
-Add veggies to rice and add Italian herbs.

Cranberry Herb Rice

- 1 cup water
- 1/2 cup rice
- 2 Tbsp butter
- 1/2 tsp salt
- 1/4 cup dried cranberries
- 2 tsp basil
- 1/4 cup walnut pieces

-Add water, rice, butter, and salt. Bring to a boil and simmer for 15 minutes.
-Stir in cranberries, basil, and walnut pieces. Let stand covered for 5 minutes.

DESSERTS

- Bread desserts
- Cakes
- Chocolate yummies
- Fruit delights
- Pies & tarts

BREAD DESSERTS

Why do cruisers choose to anchor right on top of each other? I understand in crowded anchorages when you have to wedge yourself into tight areas, but I am talking about the times that you have an entire beach or bay available and the next person comes right next to you and anchors anyways. I am sure subconsciously it has to do with the idea that either 1) the person there knows something you do not, 2) obviously it is safe where they are, or 3) as a species we like to be in groups. That does not mean the person already there wants you right next to them though!

When I was cruising the Bahamas, I anchored behind Great Guana Cay in the Exumas. This island is five miles long and the entire side I was on is 10-15 feet deep in perfect sand. I found a perfect place to have some solitude for a few days and I loved the spot I chose. It was nice and calm, the beach was beautiful, and there was not a boat within sight. Well guess what? Not two hours later another cruiser came up and anchored less than 200 feet from me. I was blown away. This guy could have anchored anywhere along this five mile stretch of empty island, but he chose to be so close we could talk from our boats.

Another time I was anchored in Anegada in the British Virgin Islands. Over the years of running charters in the BVI I have found my favorite places to anchor and Anegada is no different. I love my spot there because it is away from the mooring field, gets a little more protection from waves, and is shallow enough no one uses it. Well one time I had just anchored and was putting all the sails away and getting lunch ready for my guest when a German family of three dinghied over. Apparently, they thought it was too shallow and asked me "is it safe over here?" I wanted to be a smart ass and say "nope, stuck here until I get a tow" but was nice and simply told them it was. They asked if they should move over here and I told them why I liked it and that there was plenty of room behind me in the empty bay. I guess they took that as an invitation to drop their anchor right behind my boat instead of farther back in the bay. My guest got them back though by blowing their new conch horn until almost bedtime...of course by that time I had a headache from hearing that stupid horn. ☐

My friend Kristina always reminds me of the time her family was aboard, and I took them to a secluded beach they loved so much we stayed two nights. It is on the west coast of Vieques five miles from Puerto Rico. This particular beach is two miles long, but is not your white sand, maintained, beach bar type of beach many people think of in the tropics. Instead this one has darker sand and the palm trees are growing, and falling, in a natural state. This is about as natural of a beach as you can find in such a short sail from civilization. None the less it is amazing how easily people fall in love with this beach. As the other two parts of this story start, we were the only ones along the entire beach and I had my big, floating mat out and tied to the boat, so everyone could swim, layout, relax, wrestle, and whatever else they wanted to do in paradise. Everyone was loving it when out of nowhere a power boat came in fast and anchored a hundred feet from us. Again, he could have gone anywhere on this beach, but chose to be next to us. Everyone was mystified but tried to let it go even though we could hear everything going on at their boat and vice versa. All of a sudden, the winds picked up to 30 plus knots as a thunderhead passed by and the floating mat was lifted up, ripped away from the boat, and blown away. I dove in immediately and swam the mat down, but it was a struggle swimming back with that huge thing against such a wind. I guess the other boat saw me and zipped over in their dinghy to help me pull it back to the Guiding Light. In the blink of an eye, I was glad they were anchored so close.

Just goes to show you, one minute you are lambasting someone for anchoring too close or some other form of insult, and the next you are baking them something warm in the oven as a thank you.

BANANA BREAD

- 3 Bananas
- 1/3 cup butter (melted)
- 1 cup sugar
- 1 egg
- 1 tsp vanilla
- 1 tsp baking soda
- 1/4 tsp salt
- 1 1/2 cups flour

-Mix all ingredients together with a blender.
-Bake for one hour at 350 degrees in a greased loaf pan.
-Let cool before removing from pan.

BREAD PUDDING WITH APRICOT SAUCE

- 5 cups cubed dry bread with crust
- 3 eggs
- 2 cups milk
- 3/4 cup brown sugar
- 1/2 cup sugar
- 3 Tbsp butter (melted)
- 1 Tbsp vanilla
- 1 tsp cinnamon
- 1/3 cup golden raisins
- 1/2 cup apricot preserves
- 1 1/2 Tbsp orange juice
-

-Spread bread in a greased 9x9 pan.
-Beat eggs in bowl until frothy. Add milk, brown sugar, sugar, butter, vanilla, and cinnamon. Mix well.
Stir in raisins & pour over bread. Press bread down until coated.
-Let stand for 30 minutes pressing bread occasionally to help soak them.
-Bake 325 degrees for 40 minutes until bread pudding is browned and puffy.
-Boil preserves with orange juice and serve over warm bread pudding.

CAKES

A couple years ago I had a guest spend all week talking about how good their wine cake was and how the whole family loved it. At the end of the week she insisted I write down the recipe and how it would be a big hit for my charter guests. I appreciated the offer and tested it out when I had a break in my charters a few weeks later.

I made it exactly as she told me to and I thought it was good, but not quite as good as she raved about it. The part I liked was that you could taste the wine and mixed with the nutmeg it had a wonderful spiciness to it. But if you know anything about me and cooking, I like to play around with recipes I get and see if I can make them better and/or easy since I live on a boat with limited counter and storage space.

So, the next morning as I was sailing along the south coast of St John I was mulling over different ideas and I started to wonder if rum instead of wine would be good. Then I realized that would make it a rum cake and that would start to fall into my buddy Steve's specialty.

Steve is the guy you read about in the story about making Da Lime In Da Coconut drink in the cocktail section. I first met him in the Bahamas when he, I, and four or so other boats sailed together through the Exumas. Each of us had ties to Texas somehow, so we became known as the Texas Navy in the Bahamas cruising community. I found out later that we were known on some of the cruising forums in the States also. The great thing about us all hanging out was that we did a lot of potlucks together and Steve would always bring this killer rum cake. The man could not cook anything else, but he made that rum cake so good no one could compete with it. Two years later he started running charters in the Virgin Islands, but since his future wife had not moved aboard yet he ran captain only charters just like I do. He knew he could not cook dinners like I do on my charters, so he decided to use his specialty to his advantage and have a chocolate rum cake waiting for guests when they arrived. Sounds like the perfect way to start a charter to me.....get your guest drunk off rum cake.

I tell you all this, so you understand why I could not simply turn the wine cake into a rum cake. I did not want to infringe on what had become his calling card. So, there I was quietly sailing downwind on a perfect day when my mind drifted to the mango mojito drink I came up with and serve as a drink of the day. All of a sudden it hit me, what if I make a lime and mint sauce to go on top of the rum cake? Now it is a mojito cake and totally different.

I played around with the idea and after testing it out and loving it, I made it on a charter the next week. It was a huge hit and everyone loved it. In fact, one of the guests was shoveling it in so fast and licking the plate she had the lime and mint glaze in her hair. That is when you know you have a winner on your hands!!!!!

CHOCOLATE CAKE

Cake

- 2 cups sugar
- 1 3/4 cups flour
- 3/4 cup cocoa powder
- 1 1/2 tsp baking powder
- 1 1/2 tsp baking soda
- 1 tsp salt
- 2 eggs
- 1 cup milk
- 1/2 cup vegetable oil
- 2 tsp vanilla
- 1 cup boiling water

-Mix dry ingredients together and then add all wet ingredients except water and beat on medium speed for two minutes.
-Stir in boiling water (batter will be thin) and pour into a greased 9x13 pan.
-Bake at 350 degrees for 35 minutes and cool completely before frosting.

Frosting

- 1/2 cup butter
- 2/3 cup cocoa powder
- 3 cups powder sugar
- 1/3 cup milk
- 1 tsp vanilla

-Melt butter and add cocoa.
-Alternately add powder sugar and milk, beating on medium speed.
-Stir in vanilla and frost cake once it is completely cool.

ECLAIR CAKE

- 1 small package vanilla instant pudding
- 1 3/4 cups whole milk
- 8 oz. cool whip
- 1 box graham crackers
- 3 Tbsp butter (melted)
- 3 Tbsp milk
- 3 Tbsp cocoa
- 1 cup powdered sugar

-Blend milk & vanilla pudding together. Let sit for 5 minutes before folding in Cool Whip.
-In a 9x9 pan, layer graham crackers to cover bottom of pan (shape crackers to fit nicely)
-Pour half the pudding/cool whip mixture on top and level.
-Put another layer of graham cracker to cover entire surface.
-Put the second half of pudding/cool whip mixture on top and level.
-Put the final layer of graham crackers on top with bumpy side down.
-Mix butter, milk, cocoa, and sugar together to make a glaze. Pour over top of graham crackers and smooth out nicely.
-Refrigerate for a minimum of 4 hours.

MOJITO CAKE

- 1 package yellow cake mix
- 1 small package instant vanilla pudding mix
- 4 eggs
- 1 tsp nutmeg
- 3/4 cup vegetable oil
- 3/4 cup rum
- 2 Tbsp butter
- 1/4 cup lime juice
- 2 cups powder sugar
- 1/4 cup fresh mint leaves (pulverized) -or- 1 Tbsp dry mint leaves

-Mix cake, pudding, eggs, nutmeg, oil, and rum with a mixer. Pour into a greased bunt pan.
-Bake for 25 minutes at 350 degrees.
-Make glaze with butter, lime juice, sugar, and mint.
-Once cake is cooled flip unto a serving plate and drizzle glaze over it.

CHOCOLATE YUMMIES

Joel is my best friend and boat systems guy. The man seems to know everything about all the systems I have on the boat from electrical, radio, plumbing, engines, etc. He is by far my go to guy when I have questions on any of the systems. Just beware of doing any small projects on the boat, because as he says, "within every small project is a large job trying to get out".

At the end of my second season running charters I decided it was time to replace all three of my heads (marine toilets). The boat originally had manual, salt water flushing toilets that pumped directly overboard. When I sailed it to Houston I had to install holding tanks to conform to USCG standards. The entire system was not super clean since you always had water sitting in the bowls and there was a slight smell. I was contemplating removing everything and installing simple composting toilets. The manufacturer sent me one to check out, so I had it shipped to my parents place to get their opinion also. My mother says she never thought there would be a day she would sit around the living room staring at, sitting on, and discussing the benefits of a toilet. In the end, I was convinced this was the system for my boat. My parents agreed to help me take them, along with 7-10 other boxes, to Puerto Rico where the boat was hauled out. For two days my mom cleaned the boat while I pulled out various parts of the old toilet system. Off to the side of the boat I had a growing pile of toilets, pumps, hoses, holding tanks, and other miscellaneous parts. As the pile grew my mom declared that any system had to be better than one with some much stuff attached to it. Finally, after two days of scraping my knuckles getting stuff out it was time to install the new toilets and they went in like a dream. I have had them for over five years now and still think they were the right choice due to the simplicity of the maintenance and the fact that you get no smells like other boats. But remember Joel's saying, because even though this was not a small project it was a rather simple one except the toilets sat on the original base, which made the new seat too high. The next year I had to have a fiberglass guy come in and remove the two-inch platform the toilets sat on and re-glass the area. Worth it though.

Another thing Joel always says is that it cannot be a successful job until there is the "letting of blood". I thought when he came down and helped me install new solar panels onto the top of cockpit hardtop, he would get proven wrong. Everything went so smooth it amazed both of us. We got everything lined up, mounted, and wired within a couple days and almost finished before the boat went back into the water after being dry docked for hurricane season. Since we were in the water and ahead of schedule I suggested we take the boat to Isla Palominos, which is an hour from Fajardo, Puerto Rico. I said we could get out of the marina, swim, relax, and finish the last little bit of the solar panels there. He thought that was a great idea and off we went. We finished the solar panels that afternoon and had put all the tools away without one drop of blood being spilled. Ha, I got him! That is when I noticed a small gecko, that must have missed the notice we were heading to sea, scurrying across the deck. I picked the little guy up and tossed him into the water, so he could swim ashore on a new island. Bam, bam, bam, that is when he got hammered by three fish. Poor guy.

I guess Joel is right, the project was now complete because there was a letting of blood...it just happened to not be either of our blood. Personally, I would rather just enjoy some chocolate to signify I am done with a project.

BAILEYS & WHITE CHOCOLATE TRUFFLES

- 3.5 oz vanilla wafers
- 3/4 cup white chocolate chips
- 4 Tbsp butter
- 1 1/2 Tbsp Baileys
- 1 package hot coco mix

-Crush vanilla wafers in a blender until powder.
-Melt chocolate then add butter, turn off heat, and mix well.
-Mix in Baileys and then add crumbs.
-Form into balls and roll in hot coco powder.
-Chill for a bit and then serve.

CHOCOLATE CHIP COOKIES

- 2 cups Crisco
- 1 1/2 cups sugar
- 1 1/2 cups brown sugar
- 4 eggs
- 1 Tbsp vanilla
- 5 cups flour
- 1 1/2 tsp baking soda
- 1 1/2 tsp salt
- 2 packages (12 oz) chocolate chips

-Add everything to an extra-large bowl and mix together by hand.
-Put 12 balls of about an inch each on a cookie sheet.
-Bake for 11 minutes at 375 degrees.
-Pull out of oven but leave the cookies on the cookie sheet for 7 more minutes.
-Transfer to a cooling rack for 10 minutes and then place them into a sealed container.

CHOCOLATE LASAGNA

- 1 package Oreo cookies
- 6 Tbsp melted butter
- 1 package cream cheese (softened)
- 1/4 cup sugar
- 2 Tbsp milk
- 1 tub cool whip
- 1 small package of chocolate pudding
- 1 3/4 cups + 2 Tbsp milk
- 1 1/2 cups mini chocolate chips

-Crush Oreo cookies to crumbs.
-Add butter to crumbs and pack down to form a crust in a 9x13 pan and chill.
-Mix cream cheese with mixer until fluffy then add 2 tablespoons of milk and sugar and mix well. Fold in Cool Whip and spread over crust.
-Mix pudding & milk together, let stand 5 minutes, and spread over cream cheese mixture.
-Spread remaining Cool Whip over the top of pudding and sprinkle with chocolate chips.
-Let chill for 4 hours in fridge.

FRUIT DELIGHTS

One Sunday in the Bahamas, I left Rum Cay around 8pm with the idea of sailing close haul in a 10-15 knot ENE wind to Samana Cay and arrive around 10am the next day, so I could have good light to enter the reef of this remote and uninhabited island. Well, the winds did not cooperate and were 15-20 knot from the east instead, so I had to motor sail because the wind was closer on the bow than I could sail.

During the night one of the cars on my main broke and the six-foot waves shifted a little making it dangerous to enter the reef fringed bay of Samana Cay. On top of this a cold front was only two days behind me. Therefore, I decided it would not be a good idea to make landfall at Samana and instead continued onto Mayaguana Island. Turning my 14-hour solo sail into a trip of 23 hours straight.

I don't know what it was about that day, I mean I have been in higher winds and seas and on longer passages, but I hit a pretty low emotional point on the trip. I think it happens to everyone on boats and in life, where you wonder what you are doing and why. I had thoughts of just selling the boat and going back to Colorado! I missed my family, friends, and playing soccer! I simply was not a happy camper and I just wanted to be done with the passage, take a hot shower, eat a bowl of soup, and GO TO BED!!!!

Well I did finally get to Mayaguana, but it was an hour after dark and two hours before the moon rose, so it was pitch black. Once I entered the lee of the island I found protection but had to get closer to shore due to the depth of the water. I crept closer and closer and once I was in 45 feet of water I dropped and set the anchor and was done for the night.

The next morning I started pulling the anchor up and had a bit of an issue....It was stuck and when I finally got it loose the anchor was not at the end of the chain!!!!!!! The shackle holding it on was pulled apart and bent. As you might imagine this did not help my mood from the previous day. I decided my best course of action was to take the GPS coordinates down and go 10 miles to Abrahams Bay and pay a fisherman/diver to retrieve it.

I found two guys with an air compressor to do it for only $100. Once we got to the coordinates, the first thing he grabbed was.....his fishing spear!?! He proceeded to dive down twice when I got us to the exact spot and twice he found nothing but did have a big ol' lobster on his spear. By the third attempt I was geared up and went in to "help". I only swam upwind 25 feet before I saw chain marks in the sand forming a huge arrow right to my anchor. It was right then that the fisherman was able "find" my anchor. Gee, thanks, Haha. He tied a line around the roll bar of the anchor and up it came. Once back to the Guiding Light, I asked if he was going to give me one of the lobsters since I was the one paying for the trip. He reluctantly handed one to me. Score!

I don't know why but the simple act of recovering my anchor turned my mood around. All of a sudden, a wave of contentment washed over me and lasted for months. So, if you find yourself in a funk, no matter where you are and what you are doing, things will turn around. Of course, a few prayers and some dessert always helps too!

CHERRY PASTERY

- 2 packages crescent rolls
- 1 package of cream cheese (softened)
- 2 Tbsp butter (divided and melted)
- 1/4 cup sugar
- 2 tsp lemon juice
- 1 can cherry pie filling
- 1 egg white (beaten)
- 1/2 cup powder sugar
- 1/2 tsp vanilla
- 1 Tbsp milk

-In a greased 9x9 pan use one of the cans of crescent rolls on the bottom and sides.
-Mix the cream cheese, half the butter, sugar, and lemon juice together and smear it on top of the crescent rolls.
-Spread the pie filling on top of the cream cheese mixture.
-Cover everything with the other crescent roll package.
-Brush the egg white over the top of the crescent roll to help with the browning.
-Bake for 20-25 minutes at 350 degrees.
-Mix the powder sugar, other butter, vanilla, and milk together to make an icing.
-Once the pastry has cooled down some drizzle with the icing and serve.

BANANA FOSTERS

- 2 bananas per person
- 4 Tbsp butter
- 1/4 cup brown sugar
- 1/4 cup rum
- 2 tsp lemon juice
- 1 tsp nutmeg
- 1 tsp cinnamon
- whipped cream

-In a large skillet heat the butter under medium high heat.
-Slice the bananas length wise and then in half and sauté on both sides.
-Once done stack 8 pieces in each bowl with two one way, two the other, etc..
-In the hot skillet put the brown sugar, rum, lemon juice, nutmeg, and cinnamon.
-Cook until the sauce thickens and then spoon over the bananas.
-Top with a dollop of whipped cream.

PINEAPPLE SOUFFLE

- 1 can crushed pineapple
- 1 cup sugar
- 3 eggs
- 3 Tbsp flour
- 4 slices of bread (thicker is better)
- 1 stick of butter

-Mix everything into a bowl except bread and butter.
-Melt butter in pan and sauté bread on both sides until golden and crisp.
-Put two slices of bread in greased loaf pan.
-Pour half the mixture over bread.
-Put the other two slices on top and cover with the rest of mixture.
-Bake for 25 minutes at 350 degrees.

RED WINE PEARS

- 1 cup sugar
- 2 1/2 cups red wine
- 1 Tbsp cinnamon
- 1 tsp cloves
- 1 Tbsp grated orange peel
- 1/2 pear per person (peeled, cored and halved)
- 4 oz chocolate chips
- 1/2 cup heavy cream
- 3 tsp crushed mint

-Dissolve the sugar into the red wine by bringing to a boil in a large skillet.
-Add the cinnamon, cloves, and orange peels.
-Place the pear halves in the red wine and simmer for 10 minutes per side (spoon the wine over the pears periodically).
-In a small sauce pan melt the chocolate and add the cream and mint until smooth.
-Place cooked pear on a plate and drizzle chocolate over the top.

PIES & TARTS

My work attire on the boat consists of a t-shirt and shorts. They get worn and used a lot over the years and eventually have to be "retired". Sometimes this is after I contemplate how much wear they have and determine they are too shabby to continue as public clothing thus get relegated to boat project clothes. Other times nature causes an immediate retirement when the back end of the shorts fails catastrophically. Here are a few of the funniest stories of this unceremonious ending.

The first happened while I was on charter back in 2013. We docked temporarily at the Leverick Bay Marina fuel dock, in the North Sound of the British Virgin Islands, to fill with water, ice, provisions, and for my guest to walk around. While they were off shopping I filled the boat with water and then went to get the ice. The guest asked me to get four ten-pound bags and instead of carrying them two at a time I chose to pile them up and wrap my arms around all 40 pounds. Squatting down was no problem, but as soon as I strained to stand up with the ice, my shorts ripped all the way up my butt. I dropped the ice, stood straight up, covered my butt with my hands, and got the uh-oh look on my face. I looked around and realized no one else was on the dock and I still had to get the ice to the boat, so went ahead and grabbed all of it, walked down the dock with 40 pounds of ice, and my butt cheeks flapping in the wind.

The second time it happened was when I hauled the Guiding Light out of the water in Puerto Rico to store it for the 2014 hurricane season. I had some very good friends helping me out and we needed to move the dinghy about 10 feet and turn it 90 degrees. We each got on a corner and as soon as we started to lift, out my butt came through the shorts. Again, I shot straight up, covered it with my hands, turned red, and said I would be right back. My friends said let's go ahead and finish moving the dinghy and then you can change. I indicated that was not a good idea since I did not have any underwear on. At that point I had more than enough time to change, because they were too busy rolling on the ground in laugher. In fact, I still get teased about it. Nice friends huh?

The last time it happened was in early 2018 on St Thomas, USVI. My girlfriend and I were waiting at the dinghy dock for a ride out to the Guiding Light, since I had the dinghy engine disassembled and was working on it. While we were waiting, another gentleman came by with lots of stuff to load into his dinghy. I offered to help, and he graciously accepted. Of course, right there in the middle of the dock with a restaurant 10 feet away another pair of shorts gave out and left my bottom exposed to the elements. Of course, I quickly assumed the now common pose of standing with hands over my butt as I assessed the situation. The problem was this time I had nowhere to go to get new shorts, since I was still waiting on the ride back to the boat. So, there I was trying to pull my t-shirt down low enough to keep my checks from appearing until my ride arrived. When it did I needed to help hold the dinghy as we got everything in and then cast off. My girlfriend was laughing and embarrassed at the same time as she kept pulling on the shirt to cover the shorts lacking butt!

Hum, three different times my shorts have blown out. Is it possible my butt is getting too big due to all the desserts I eat? Nah, I am sure it is only because the shorts have gotten worn out.

KEY LIME MOOSSE

- 1 can sweeten condensed milk
- 1/2 cup key lime juice
- 1 package cool whip
- 1 graham cracker crust

-Mix milk and lime juice with an electric mixer until fluffy.
-Fold in cool whip and put into crust.
-Chill and serve.

PEPPERMINT PIE

- 1 Oreo cookie crumb crust
- 4 cups marshmallows
- 1/2 cup milk
- 1 cup heavy cream (whipped)
- 1/2 cup crushed peppermint candy

-Cook on stovetop 3 cups of the marshmallows and milk. Stir until smooth and chill until slightly thick.
-Fold in cream, 1 cup marshmallows, and peppermint.
-Spoon this onto of the crust and refrigerate for 4 hours.
-Sprinkle top of the pie with more candy cane bits as decoration.

TROPICAL FRUIT TART

- 1/2 cup sugar
- 2 Tbsp water
- 3 Tbsp butter
- 2 Tbsp whipping cream
- 3 cans tropical fruit (apricots are really good also)
- 1 graham cracker crust (or 6 little crusts)

-Place sugar and water in a pan and stir over medium heat until dissolved.
-Continue without stirring until the syrup is amber in color.
-Add the butter and cream and stir over low heat until dissolved.
-Pack the fruit tightly into the pie crust.
-Pour the caramel over the fruit.
-Bake for 20 minutes at 400 degrees and serve warm.

WHITE CHOCOLATE CRANBERRY TART

- 1/3 cup + 1 Tbsp shortening
- 1 1/2 cup flour
- 1/4 tsp salt
- 3 Tbsp water
- 1 cup sugar
- 2 eggs
- 1/4 cup butter (half a stick)
- 2 tsp vanilla
- 6 oz white chocolate
- 1 package dried cranberries

-Mix shortening, 1 cup flour, salt, and water together to form dough for the crust. Press into a deep-dish pie pan or roll out and put in pan.
-Mix sugar, eggs, melted butter, vanilla, and 1/2 cup flour in a bowl and mix together.
-Add white chocolate and cranberries, mix together, pour in pie crust, and level it out.
-With a butter knife trim the crust away right above the filling level.
-Bake for 40 minutes at 350 degrees.

BREAKFAST

Everyone has to do it at some point and today is one of my days. Laundry on a boat is a bit different than on shore. Mostly because of the different ways to do it and the effort and resources involved with each way. Some boats throw the dirty clothes in a bucket or cooler and let the action of sailing agitate the clothes clean and then rinse them off and hang them out to dry. Other boats have small washing machines aboard. The idea is fantastic, but the problem is the amount of water used per load, which is a big deal when you have to carry or make your own water.

I personally just go to the laundromat like you would on shore...kind of. For me I have to pack everything up and then load the bags into the dinghy. After a weeklong charter with six guests and all my personal clothes I can have so many bags piled on the bow I look like Santa Claus delivering gifts as I arrive at the dinghy dock. At some docks I may be the only boat, making it easy to unload the bags, but here in Charlotte Amalie the dock is usually two, three, or even four dinghies deep. So now I have to play a game combining leap frog, throwing a medicine ball, and dodge ball to get the bags of dirty laundry from my dinghy into the next dinghy to get to the next one to get on the dock. Ahhhh, made it. Now it is a simple matter of walking to the laundromat, which I have found anywhere from right at the marina to over a mile away. Of course, I am not smart enough to bring a cart and too cheap to pay the taxi the ridiculous amount to go such a short distance, so I put bags on my back like backpacks one on top of another while carrying a few also. I'm sure I look like a camel or about to start a long-distance trek, but I only made it ten feet or so before I looked for another option. Thank goodness for shopping carts. Can you image the look I get pushing a shopping cart down the street with almost a hundred pounds of laundry? Me neither because I am too busy trying to control the four wheeled demon buggy determined to have one of the wheels go off in a different direction.

Here in the USVI a regular washer is only $2 (double and triple loaders are comparable at $4 and $6), but some locations in The Bahamas I saw up to $8 a load for a regular size washer (needless to say those are reserved by cruisers for only the direst of clean clothes situations). After the hour and a half to four hours it takes to get everything washed, dried, and folded I get to reverse the process. Of course, this time I want to be very careful not to splash salt water on my nice, clean laundry. Wait a minute is that rain? Well, that is timing for you. Hurry up and get back to the boat!

It sounds like a lot of effort and I do miss having the washer and dryer in my basement, so I can do other things at the same time. But let me tell you it is so worth doing laundry while living aboard a boat when I am able to crawl into bed between clean, crisp, dry sheets and drift off to sleep for the night and then wake up aboard a boat and have breakfast while looking out over the sea and amazing beach I am anchored at.

Nowadays, I got smart and simply have a guy come pick it all up, wash it for me, and then deliver it back to the boat later in the afternoon. All I have to do is sit back and enjoy my breakfast! Totally worth it!!!

BREAKFAST DINNER

- Hollandaise sauce
- 2 egg yolks
- 2 Tbsp lemon juice
- 1 stick butter (cold)
- 1 lb bacon
- 2 sweet potatoes (diced)
- 1 onion (diced)
- 4 Tbsp maple syrup
- 12 eggs

-Make Hollandaise sauce by combining egg yolks and lemon juice in a small sauce pan and put over very low heat. Add stick of butter and stir continually until butter is melted. If sauce curdles, add 1 Tbsp water and stir until smooth.
-Fry bacon and set aside but keep warm.
-Sauté sweet potato and onion in bacon drippings until soft.
-Transfer to a bowl with a third of the bacon crumbled up and the syrup to make a hash and keep warm.
-cook eggs as desired.
-Serve by putting a helping of the hash on a plate, add two eggs on top, spoon a serving of Hollandaise sauce over eggs, and top with two strips of bacon.

CITRUS CANTALOUPE SOUP

- 1 cantaloupe (skinned & chunked)
- 1/2 cup orange juice
- 1 cup vanilla yogurt
- 2 Tbsp honey
- Garnish with yogurt, mint leaves, and nutmeg

-Blend everything and chill.
-Garnish with a dollop of yogurt and mint leaf and then sprinkle with nutmeg.

Crepes

- 1 1/2 cup flour
- 1 Tbsp sugar
- 1/2 tsp baking powder
- 1/2 tsp salt
- 2 cups milk
- 2 Tbsp butter (melted)
- 1/2 tsp vanilla
- 2 eggs

-Mix all ingredients together.
-Pour 1/3 cup of batter onto a hot pan and rotate until thin film covers bottom.
-Cook until bubbles form and then flip with a spatula. Stack on a plate.

Filling

- 1 package cream cheese (softened)
- 3 Tbsp brown sugar
- 1 egg

-Mix everything well and put glob on each crepe, wrap up, and place in baking pan.
-Bake for 10 minutes at 350 degrees and serve with fruit and whip cream.

Well folks, I hope I helped add to your dinners with both new meals and entertaining stories you can share with each other.

As Porky Pig would say, ""Th-th-th-that's all folks!"

May you have fair winds and following seas.

- Capt Shane

Made in the USA
Lexington, KY
16 February 2019